Horse's Hicc

Horse had the hiccups.

"Stand on your head
like this," said Pig.

2

3

So Horse stood on his head,
but he still had the hiccups.

4

5

"Hold your breath
like this," said Sheep.

6

7

So Horse held his breath,
but he still had the hiccups.

8

9

"Pat your tummy
and rub your head
like this," said Goat.

10

11

So Horse patted his tummy
and rubbed his head,
but he still had the hiccups.

12

13

Owl swooped by.
"SCREEEEECH!"

Horse was frightened.

14

15

"My hiccups are gone!"
said Horse. "Thank you, Owl."